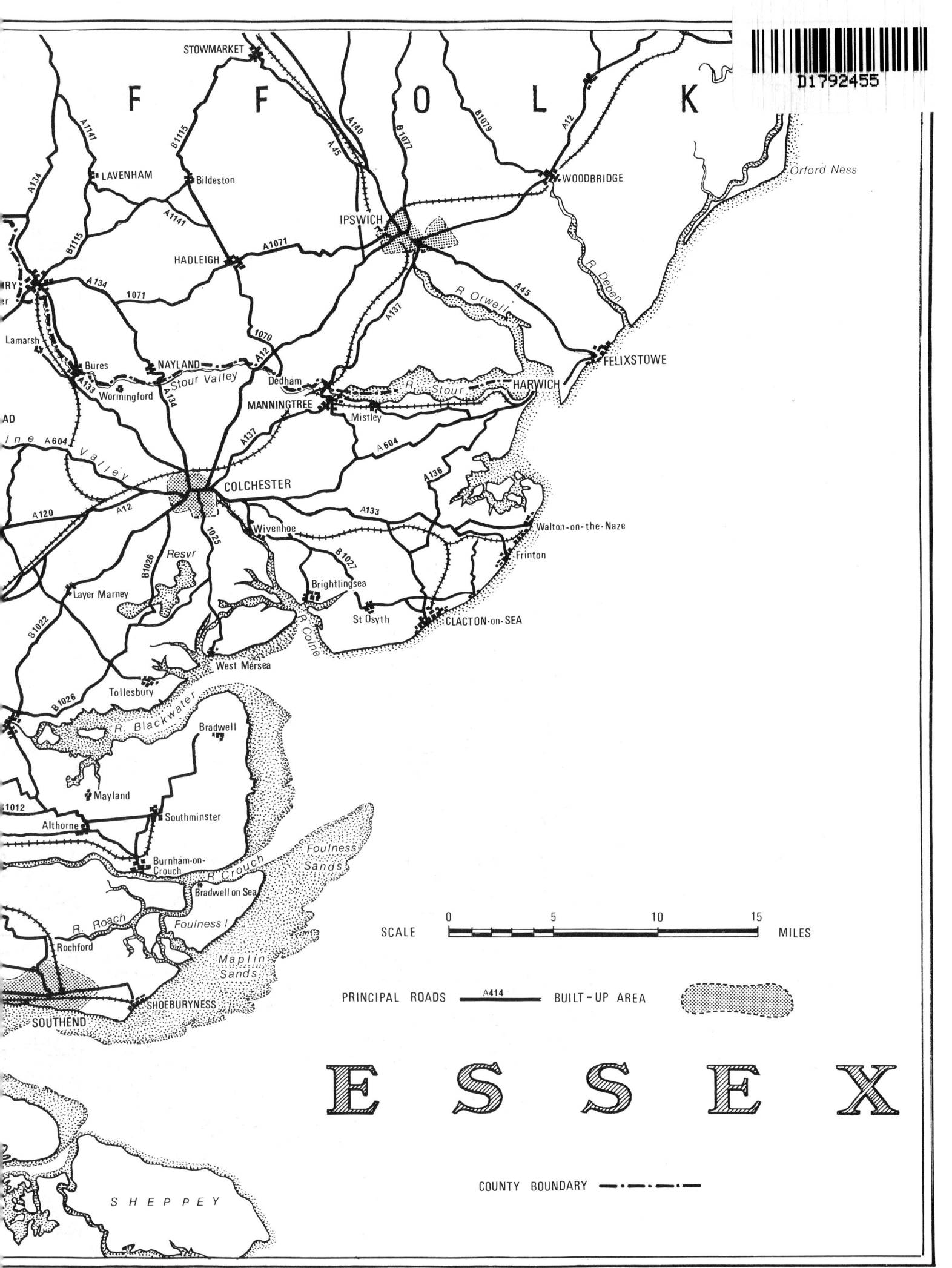

England in cameracolour
Essex

England in cameracolour
Essex

PHOTOGRAPHS BY JOHN BETHELL
TEXT BY FRANCESCA BARRAN

LONDON

A member of the Ian Allan Group

Bibliography

The Buildings of England: Essex, Nikolaus Pevsner, Penguin Books.
Essex in the Days of Old, John T. Page, William Andrews & Co (1898).
The Pattern of English Building, Alec Clifton-Taylor, Faber & Faber (1972).
English History from Essex Sources 1750-1900, A. F. J. Brown, County Council of Essex (1952).
An Anthology of Essex collected by Isabel Lucy & Beatrice Mary Gould, Marston Sampson Low & Co Ltd (1911).
Essex by Marcus Crouch, B. T. Batsford (1969).
Essex Highways Byways and Waterways C. R. B. Barrett, Lawrence & Bullen (1892).
The King's England: Essex, Arthur Mee, Hodder & Stoughton (1940).

First published 1984

ISBN 0 86364 026 5

All rights reserved. No part of this book may be reproduced or transmitted in any form or by any means, electronic or mechanical, including photo-copying, recording or by any information storage and retrieval system, without permission from the Publisher in writing.

Photographs © John Bethell 1984

© Town & County Books Ltd 1984

Published by Town & County Books Ltd, Shepperton, Surrey; and printed in Italy by Graphische Betriebe Athesia, Bolzano

Introduction

'I come not from Heaven, but from Essex'
William Morris, *Dream of John Ball*

Essex is the eighth largest county in England and presents as varied a face as any. It includes the huge conurbation of East London but no other city of any size. The largest town outside the orbit of London is Southend and even that is not big with a population of only 157,000, and the county town of Chelmsford has only 139,000 inhabitants. The great built-up area along the north bank of the Thames includes the Ford works at Dagenham, the largest in Britain, the great port at Tilbury, the refinery of Shell Haven, and the chemical works on Canvey Island. And in the heartland of rural north Essex is the ever growing airport at Stansted. All this is in striking contrast to the rest of the county. Here the most characteristic landscapes are the river estuaries of the Colne, the Blackwater, the Crouch and the Thames with the large flat islands of Mersea, Foulness and Canvey lying near their mouths.

Although there are no great heights — at no point does the land reach an altitude of even 500ft — yet the whole aspect of the county is rolling. Geologically, Essex is a chalk bowl overlayed with clay, rich and fertile in the north, and gravelly in the south on the land bordering the Thames.

The great forest which once covered Essex was preserved by successive kings through the Middle Ages as a royal hunting ground. The latter-day forests of Epping, Hatfield and Hainault are only a small fragment of what once existed, but are none the less precious because of what has gone.

The earliest record of man comes from the coastal region around Clacton where flint tools dating from 400,000 BC have been excavated. In early times the dense forest of the hinterland must have seemed uninviting to settlers, indeed the earliest traces of any agricultural activity do not appear until the middle of the fourth millenium BC, which indicates that Essex was the last area in Southern Britain to be settled by a farming community.

Soon after Julius Caesar's exploratory campaign the region, which had been ruled by the Trinovates, was overrun by the Catuvellauni who established their capital at Colchester, naming it Camulodonum after their god of war, Camulos. As a strategic centre for the region, it commanded the land routes north, west and south and to the sea through its trading port on the Colne. Its advantages were fully apparent to Claudius who came in 49AD to receive the submission of 11 native kings. The colonia he established was sacked and its inhabitants massacred in the great revolt of the Iceni in 61AD led by Boudicca, or Boadicea as we once all called her. However the land was quickly retaken, a new colonia was built on the site of the old and walls were raised about it.

The third century AD saw the advent of Saxon pirate raids which necessitated the construction of forts along what the Romans called the Saxon Shore. Bradwell is the only example of this type of defensive work in the county and there is evidence that this fort was inhabited until the fifth century, that is until the departure of the Romans. Their departure was swiftly followed by the arrival of the East Saxons who naturally gravitated towards the areas which had been cultivated by the Romans. Colchester they left entirely alone as they tended to despise urban life.

The coming of Christianity to Essex is marked by one important relic, the chapel of St Peter at Bradwell Juxta Mare. While most Saxon building would have been of wood, this church built on the ruins of the Saxon shore fort used Roman brick, tile and stone which have withstood the intervening 13 centuries. Miraculously one timber building has also survived from Saxon times. This is the little log cabin church of St Andrew at Greensted which recent experiment has dated at c850AD.

Colchester was again given strategic prominence about 1085 when William the Conqueror chose to build the largest keep in Europe there. Norman churches survive in the county at St Botolph in Colchester, in ruins, and magnificently, though much altered, at Waltham Abbey. There the nine bays of the nave are punctuated by massive circular piers incised with geometrical decoration. Another great Norman keep is that of Castle Hedingham, the most complete keep of the period to survive anywhere in Europe. In monastic times the most powerful order in Essex was the Augustinian whose first house in Britain was St Essex Botolph in Colchester. Other houses in the county included St Osyth and Waltham itself.

Trees — especially oak trees — and the timber they produce have long made a major contribution to the Essex scene. Woodland and coppice not only add variety to the landscape, they often define the skyline in the flatter areas. Their timber was used for almost all church building until the late Middle Ages both for structure and decoration — the county boasts many finely carved porches, towers and belfries. Apart from the hugely ostentatious Audley End, most domestic building was also in timber until the 18th century and even after that most cottage and vernacular building was in wood, timber framing with wattle and daub infill.

The first bricks made in Britain were made in Essex and many were also imported through Essex ports. Little Coggeshall, not 12 miles from Colchester, has the distinction of possessing the earliest non-Roman brick building in Britain. It is part of the former Cistercian Abbey and dates from 1190. Essex boasts many remarkable brick buildings, but none finer than Layer Marney Towers, the great gatehouse of the Marney family near Colchester where terracotta and Renaissance ornament were first seen in the county. Brick nogging — the infilling of timber frame buildings with brick in place of the original wattle and daub — was an expedient of the 17th century when competent daubers were hard to find. In utilitarian buildings like the great barn at Cressing Temple the bricks are laid in straight courses but sometimes a decorative effect was achieved by setting the bricks diagonally as at Paycockes in Coggeshall.

Flints which are found freely here in the upper layers of the chalk were first used as tools and a keen trade in them existed from prehistoric times. By the mid-13th century they were being used decoratively in building. The split gleaming black flints were placed in regular courses to face a building. By the beginning of the 14th century flints were being cut and set in patterns in combination with stone and brick. This made an agreeable appearance as well as strengthening the flint wall. Flints with their charmingly irregular shapes need to be imbedded in a great quantity of mortar and Essex, in particular Harwich, produced the famous Roman cement. It was made from stones dredged from the rocks in Harwich harbour baked in kilns and ground to a fine powder which when mixed with water made a smooth and durable mortar. The trade in cement took it to cities throughout the United Kingdom and the civilised world and flourished until the 19th century.

Timber frame buildings were, of course, the most common form of construction throughout the entire country until the 16th century. Only in Kent, Sussex and Essex, however, can one now find examples in any numbers of half-timbered houses dating from before 1500. Examples though much restored, can be seen in Saffron Walden at the former Sun Inn and at the Guildhall in Thaxted. Glamorous half-timbered buildings like the Old King's Head in Chigwell, also much restored, date from the 17th century.

Half-timbered houses were frequently 'pargetted' — that is decorated with plaster in which patterns were incised. The earliest forms of pargetting were stick and combed work, the wet plaster being simply pricked or dragged, but in the 18th century much more elaborate work was done particularly in Suffolk and Essex. A most exuberant example can be seen at the Sun Inn, Saffron Walden.

Weather-boarding is a common alternative to plaster in parts of Essex and first became popular in the 18th century. It is a modest material seen mainly on cottages, barns and especially on mills. The cheapest roofing material was thatch and as such it was mainly used for barns, cottages and small houses. The best quality of thatch is made from reed and limited quantities of it are produced in the tidal estuaries of the Essex coast. Inferior but more common thatch is of long straw and here again Essex produces some of the better quality varieties which is cut from rye. In the absence of any stone a more durable roofing material was made from baked clay tiles — pantiles. Tile making was reintroduced in the 18th century and its much greater durability and considerably greater resistance to fire ensured its popularity. Tiles, like bricks, were made wherever suitable clay could be dug — and this accounts for the great variety of colours that we find around Essex.

From the Middle Ages the north of the county had enjoyed a thriving trade based on the production of wool. The first towns to profit from Essex sheep were Maldon and Colchester which exported the wool to the Low Countries. Edward I took vigorous action to stem the export by bringing Flemish craftsmen over to establish a cloth industry here. The rivers of Essex provided the power to drive the mills and prosperous centres of the cloth industry were established along the Stour, the Colne and the Blackwater at Braintree, Coggeshall, Hedingham, Halstead, Colchester and Dedham. The decline in this trade during the 18th century is not easily explained but the effects were devastating upon Essex. A new trade in the manufacture of imitation silk was warmly welcomed when it first appeared at the end of that century and firms from Spitalfields in London moved out to set up business at the former cloth centres. Some of these manufacturers are still in production today, notably Courtaulds' at Halstead.

Along the coast and up the wide river estuaries, seafaring in all its forms provided the principal livelihood. Fishermen had often to eke out a miserable living by engaging in the more profitable business of contraband, — their intimate knowlege of the shallow water and shifting mud banks frequently making pursuit by the authorities well nigh impossible. Shipbuilding, as with other industries, tended to be on a small scale although the east coast ports were bound to supply a certain number of ships for the Kings' Navies in return for a variety of privileges. Such charters existed for Harwich, Maldon and Brightlingsea — the latter being part of the Cinque Ports complex — the only one outside Kent and Sussex.

Essex agriculture by the 18th century was progressive and prosperous. Enclosure, though frequently unjust resulted in greatly increased productivity, and easier transport resulting from the road improvements under the 'turnpike' system meant that Essex farmers could supply the enormous and growing market of London. Arthur Young, the pioneer agronomist, visiting the county in 1771 was impressed by the enlightened practice of the Essex farmers. He found that they did more to improve their soil than any other group of farmers he had observed. The Napoleonic Wars forced up the price of all farm produce but the subsequent peace brought low prices and consequent poverty and depression to the farming population. Throughout the 19th century farm prices were low and the majority of farm labourers found it hard to scratch a living. Many left the land to get jobs in the industrialised south of the county and others emigrated to Canada and Australia. It was not until just before World War 2 that the picture began to improve and it is only in very recent years that Essex land has commanded the prices it does today.

For the carriage of people and agricultural produce Essex relied not only on the turnpike roads but also, very heavily, on its rivers. The Chelmer was made navigable from Chelmsford to Maldon, and the Roding from Barking to Ilford. Then, in 1848, the first stretch of branch line railway was opened from Braintree to Maldon. Typically it was for the transportation of agricultural produce that it was chiefly welcomed and almost immediately the advantage was seen of extending the railway to the great centre of grain production at Saffron Walden.

As we have seen, the 18th century was a time of considerable prosperity for a great many in Essex. This prosperity brought leisure and the demand for fashionable amusement. Early attempts to popularise sea bathing at Wivenhoe and Mistley met with little success — but Southend, which first began to receive visitors for sea bathing in 1790, soon achieved prominence and popularity. The Essex coast seaside resorts continued to be developed throughout the 19th century notably at Walton-on-the-Naze, Clacton and later at Frinton.

Long before sea-bathing became popular, the Essex coast attracted dozens of sportsmen in pursuit of the vast numbers of wildfowl which frequented all the river estuaries. These same estuaries also provided an ideal habitat for the oyster — a dish which was formerly much more commonplace than it is today and great barrels of oysters were sent daily to London for the consumption of the ordinary people.

The 20th century has added as much or more than it has detracted from the beauties of Essex. For there is a strange eerie beauty in the great chimneys and cooling towers of Bradwell atomic station, West Thurrock power station or the Shell refinery. Frinton with its large seaside houses for the prosperous middle classes, built in the free and easy manner of Voysey, full of comfort and picturesqueness are certainly a charming addition to the Essex scene. Townsend's church at Great Warley is pretty too but glowing and exciting as well.

Essex nowadays presents us with two contrasting faces — the urbanised south and the rural north. Both are deeply connected with London the first as an overspill for industrial London, the second as a retreat from this same noisy bustling workaday world. One is a workshop the other a playground. Essex is a cheerful, prosperous county much given over to the pursuit of pleasure and that would appear to have been its character from the Middle Ages. Where the kings of England hunted and the commoners shot the wild fowl and ate the oysters is now the happy recreation ground of the Londoner. Today thousands walk and picnic, fish and ride in the remnants of Epping's royal forest. Similar numbers swim and eat ices or play the fruit machines on the piers of Clacton and Southend, or sail their boats out of Burnham or West Mersea.

William Camden wrote in *Britannia* (1586) a description of Essex which, bar the saffron, one would have few quarrels with addressing to the northern half of the county today:

'Essex is a country of great breadth, very fruitful, abounding in Saffron, very well stored with wood, and exceedingly rich.'

Francesca Barran,
1984

Stratford Watermills The earliest mills on this site belonged to the Cistercian Abbey of Stratford Langthorne of which nothing now remains. They are famous in literature for here it was that Chaucer's Prioress learnt her French:

'And Frenssh she spak ful faire and fetisly
After the scole of Stratford atte Bowe
For Frenssh of Parys wast to hire
unknowe'

In 1730 the mills fell into the hands of a distillery in which guise they continue to operate, belonging now to Messrs Nicholson's. Our photograph shows the clock tower, a polygonal open wooden belfry on an octagonal brick base with pretty Gothic windows of 1753. This is attached to the clock mill built in 1817. The great chimneys of the pair of drying kilns have an impressively bulky outline against the sky. The clock mill has three waterwheels and 14 pairs of grinding stones in addition to the drying kilns.

The River Thames at Silvertown This is Essex within London. The dockland with all the scars of the heavy wartime bombing has a romance about it now which it can never have had in its heyday. Containerisation has taken the trade to new ports like Tilbury and Felixstowe and there are few great ships now to tie up beside the vast warehouses of Tate & Lyle and Spiller's Millenium Mills. While we may regret the passing of our trading empire we can reflect that just 150 years ago this was open countryside with marshy foreshore, a haven for wildfowl feeding on the slow moving Thames. Coller in *The People's History of Essex*, published in 1861, paints a fair picture of the arrival of this busy traffic: 'It has, in fact, become a busy suburb of the metropolis, which has rubbed off its once rural character. Its little hamlets have grown into large towns. Fields over which the plough passed a quarter of a century ago are covered with workshops and teeming factories. On its river bank have risen up the largest ship building works in the world. Its quiet creek and marshland have been converted into mighty docks, furnishing a haven and a home for commerce for all countries of the earth'.

In the background of our photograph appears the great Thames barrier completed in November 1982 and raised to meet its first flood emergency in February 1983. It is the largest such barrier in the world, and took eight years to build at a cost of £435million.

Rainham Hall The southeast corner of Essex between the disused Thames docks and the industrial hinterland is an unlovely area but suddenly you leave the rows and rows of 1930s semi-detached houses surrounding the Ford works at Dagenham and find yourself in a perfect village street. Rainham church is a complete late Norman church, a rarity in this county, and beside it, behind an impressive ironwork screen stands Rainham Hall. It is a most sumptuous red brick house with rich stone quoins dating from 1729 — a house that is eminently liveable inside. The rooms are small and wainscotted and only the staircase with its twisted balusters is of the same grandeur as the exterior. Behind the house lies the stable courtyard, and dovecot. It belongs to the National Trust and can be seen on written application to the tenant.

Tilbury This Thames-side port has a distinguished place in British naval history. It was from here that Queen Elizabeth reviewed her fleet preparing to meet the approaching Spanish armada in 1588 and addressed them in her famous and magnificent words: 'I know I have the body of a weak and feeble woman but I have the heart and stomach of a king and a king of England too: and think foul scorn that Parma or Spain, or any Prince of Europe, should dare to invade the borders of my realm'.

A century later another invasion threatened, this time from the Dutch and French. To prepare for it a fort was built here by Sir Bernard de Gomme, a military engineer under Charles II. The gateway to this fort is a splendid affair. The bottom half is in the mode of a triumphal arch and the upper storey has an empty niche and a segmental pediment. To the left and right are a pair of richly carved military trophies sporting cannon, armour and flags. The fort itself was largely remodelled in the 19th century and refitted in 1913.

The Shell Oil Refinery, Shellhaven Towering up above the flat Essex marshes rise the chimney stacks and processing units of the Shell oil refinery. This huge installation was built in the 1950s to take advantage of the deep water available in the estuary at this point enabling very large tankers to discharge their cargoes of crude oil from the Persian Gulf or West Africa while moored alongside the jetty. Contrary to popular belief, the name Shellhaven has no connection with the Shell company but arises from the fact that at this point the tidal currents set into the shore carrying with them and depositing on the beach large quantities of sea shells which were used in medieval times and even in the 18th century for making mortar. After they had acquired the site the Company found that on all old maps the area was designated by this very suitable name.

Great Warley Church, near Brentwood The church of St Mary the Virgin at Great Warley may come to the unsuspecting visitor as one of the great surprises of Essex. Hardly a typical village church, it was built by Charles Harrison Townsend in 1904. The church lies in a secluded churchyard surrounded by trees. The outside is roughcast in the mode made popular by Voysey and it sports a pretty bell turret. Inside there is a feast of colour amid dimly glowing silver. The nave is tunnel vaulted and running in bands round the vault are panels of beaten silver with repoussé decoration from the international arts and crafts repertoire of stylised lilies and trees. The rood screen is a particularly delicate work in bronze. The arches are formed of stylised flowering trees, the work of William Reynolds Stephens. Curiously enough the old parish church of Great Warley is scarcely 50 years the senior of St Mary the Virgin. It is a ruin now with little remaining of Teulon's church save the west tower, a High Victorian coarse structure of yellow and red brick.

Hadleigh Castle Standing in a situation of natural advantage on a spur of land above the marshes on the north side of the Thames, Hadleigh Castle was built by Hubert de Burgh, Earl of Kent. He was a man of lowly birth but great administrative ability and, in an age of consistent double dealing, a man of outstanding if misguided loyalty. He supported King John against the barons and was the effective regent during the minority of Henry III. On his downfall, brought about by the jealousy of the barons, the castle passed into royal hands and was largely rebuilt by that great castle builder, Edward III.

The ruins are famous as the subject of one of Constable's most dramatic paintings though the actual remains are somewhat disappointing. The southeast tower is the tallest surviving, standing three storeys high with slit windows and chimney flues. The extensive masonry surroundings are the remains of the west, north and east curtain walls, and in the foreground of the photograph, the bases of four circular towers all open towards the bailey.

Southend-on-Sea Southend-on-Sea has by far the largest population of any town in Essex and yet it is a place of comparatively slight historical importance in the annals of the county. Until 200 years ago there was probably little here save a few fisherman's cottages. All this changed in the early years of George III's reign with the advent of the vogue for sea-bathing. A journal of 1768 records 'A scheme is on foot to render Southend a convenient place for bathing, the situation being esteemed the most agreeable and convenient for that purpose on the Essex coast'. However the scheme foundered until a visit in 1804 by Queen Caroline and the Princess Charlotte gave it the necessary impetus. Disraeli stayed here in 1833 and for a while enjoyed an affair with the beautiful and flighty Lady Sykes, his 'Henrietta Temple'. He wrote glowing reports of the place: 'I can answer for Southend being very pretty' . . . 'I live solely on snipe and ride a great deal. You could not have a softer climate or sunnier skies than this much-abused Southend'. Only a few years before the dramatic increase in the population following the development of Cliff Town in 1859, Southend was still being described as a quiet place for quiet people.

Not so now, the 42 miles distance that it lies from London is sufficient explanation, when taken with the acknowledgedly fine climate, to explain its popularity as a commuter town and retirement home. It is close enough too for a day out for thousands of Londoners each summer.

Burnham-on-Crouch Here the Crouch, which near its head is a most insignificant stream, swells out to a magnificent estuary half a mile wide providing the premier sailing base on the east coast. At almost any time of the year the river will be full of small craft weaving and criss-crossing, in numbers so great as to be almost impossible to count. Controlling some of all this sailing activity is the Royal Corinthian Yacht Club, the tall broad white modern building in the centre background of the photograph.

Although it lacks any great architectural merit, the little town is worth a visit to anyone who has ever enjoyed or hankered after 'messing about in boats'. Here the land and sea meet more successfully than almost anywhere else in Essex. Too often the sea shore is composed of wide mud beach or marsh, but here the little terrace of colour washed cottages on the quay provide just the right note.

The parish church of St Mary stands almost a mile north of the town, until the Dissolution it belonged to nearby Dunmow Priory. Burnham was a wool-port and where there were wealthy wool merchants you invariably find, as here, a lavishly decorated church. It also benefited from the patronage of Thomas Ratcliff, Lord Fitzwalter whose family had been patrons of Dunmow Priory which they acquired after the Dissolution.

St Peter's-on-the-Wall, Bradwell-on-Sea
In 653 Cedd, a disciple of St Aidan from Lindisfarne, was sent to the East Saxons by the Northumbrian king Oswy. He landed at the Saxon Shore fort of Othona and the ruins of the Roman fort must have provided some shelter on this inhospitable shore. It seems certain that he built his church here, the same building that we see in the photograph. The isolated position, the firm foundations on the Roman walls and the solid construction have all played a part in ensuring the remarkable survival of the Chapel. It stands at the northeast corner of the large parish and served as a chapel-of-ease to the parish church, the rector being bound to provide a priest to say mass there on Sundays, Wednesdays and Fridays. In 1442 a jury was empanelled to enquire into its condition. At that time it had both a chancel and nave as well as a small tower containing two bells. The chancel and nave, at least, were repaired by the rector and parish. The church is built almost entirely of Roman materials, brick, ashlar and septaria. The west window and doorway shown here, are all part of the original 7th century building. It is a most moving place, lashed by the east wind off the North Sea, and a fitting memorial to the heroic spirit of the early Christian church.

St Thomas's Church, Bradwell Mainly built in the 14th century, though the brick west tower dates from 1706, St Thomas's church and nearby Bradwell Lodge were the scene of one of the more curious stories of eccentric vicars. Henry Bate, afterwards the Rev Sir Henry Bate-Dudley bought the advowson of Bradwell in the year 1781 for the sum of £1,500. He had already achieved considerable notoriety when, after taking holy orders, he had been involved in a scuffle at Vauxhall in 1773. He later became a journalist, first as editor of the *Morning Post*, but on quarrelling with the proprietors he set up three new journals, *The Morning Herald*, *Courier de l'Europe* and *The English Chronicle*. These occasioned him further trouble with the law when he was committed for 12 months for publishing a libel on the Duke of Richmond. Bate-Dudley spent five years from 1792 as curate of Bradwell and while there he spent some £28,000 on reclaiming land and improving the church and rectory. The former rectory, now Bradwell Lodge has a new south façade by John Johnson, while the interior was extensively refurbished probably by Robert Adam himself. During this period the curate and his wife were painted by Gainsborough. In 1797 the rector of Bradwell died and Bate-Dudley presented the living to himself. Unfortunately for him he was overruled by the Bishop of London and the presentation of the living lapsed. Although he later received preferment in Ireland and inherited the baronetcy, he must still have smarted for the loss of Bradwell and the money he had expended on it.

Maldon Quay Maldon stands on a hill above the confluence of the Rivers Chelmer and Blackwater at the point where the Blackwater widens into an estuary. It is one of the most ancient towns in the county. In 913, during the building and fortification of Witham, Edward the Elder lay here. In 920 Maldon suitably fortified by the same monarch withstood a Danish invasion, but in 993 another Danish attack met with more success despite the doughty resistance put up by Byrhtnoth and his son and nephew as related in a contemporary Anglo-Saxon poem, *The Song of the Battle of Maldon*, a most remarkable survival of a poem of this date in the vernacular. The town of Maldon had three medieval parish churches. All Saints in the High Street is chiefly remarkable for its triangular tower, probably unique in England. The second, St Peter's at the corner of High Street and Market Hill fell into disuse and disrepair during the 17th century. Dr Plume a native of Maldon demolished all but the tower and built on the site a handsome library to house his important collection of books, an example of the state into which the church had fallen by 1700, that a leading cleric should prefer to convert a church to another use rather than to restore it to its original purpose. This building now, most suitably, provides a home for the county library.

The third church is that which appears in our photograph, St Mary's down by the riverside, its big west tower surmounted by a shingled spire providing a landmark for yachtsmen approaching up the Blackwater. At the beginning of the 17th century the original tower fell down, which, as it served as a beacon, caused much inconvenience to the river users. In 1628 a brief was issued by Charles I authorising the collection of subscriptions in various specified places to further the rebuilding. This brief met with some success as a surviving copy is endorsed 'collected in the Church of Cowley towards this briefe May 3, Two Shillings. Daniel Collins parish of Cowley'. St Mary's is the oldest of the three churches, the north wall of the nave revealing an early Norman window.

Chelmsford This ancient Essex town is frequently identified as the Roman post of Caesaromagus and Roman remains found here tend to confirm the identification.

In the 13th century the town acquired a market, a house of Blackfriars (invariably a manifestion of a town's financial success) and was made the administrative capital of the county. However it was not until 1913 that it was raised to the rank of a cathedral city. Chelmsford followed the example of Birmingham and increased the principal town church to the state of cathedral. St Mary's looks exactly what it is, the late medieval church of a prosperous market town. Its principal claim to fame is the magnificent flush work south porch.

Matters of local government were more important to the hard headed Administrators of Essex and in 1789 they commissioned John Johnson, surveyor of the county, to build the elegant office depicted here. For lack of any local stone it is built of finest Portland brought up from Dorset. The three relief panels beneath the pediment are made of Coade stone, an early composition stone invented by Mrs Coade for the inexpensive decoration of buildings in the neo-classical style. Johnson was handsomely rewarded for this work, probably his masterpiece, on completion of which he was presented with a piece of silver plate worth 100 guineas — 'As a public testimony of his integrity and professional abilities'. Of his other works for the county town the only other major survival is the elegant Moulsham Bridge. He retired from the surveyorship in 1812 at the age of 80 and received the grateful thanks of the justices 'for his long, active, faithful and meritorious services to this county during the space of more than thirty years'.

Writtle Green The survival of Writtle Green was enshrined in the Writtle and Roxwell Enclosure Award of 1871 which records 'I allot unto the parish of Writtle all those 3 pieces of land containing 2a, 3r. 2p, 18p. and 3r. to be held in trust as a place for exercise and recreation for the inhabitants of the parish and neighbourhood'.

A provision which is still enjoyed. On summer afternoons spirited games of impromptu village cricket can often be viewed here. Writtle has been almost engulfed by the dormitory of spreading Chelmsford but if you turn aside from the main A414 road you can discover the delights of what Sir Nikolaus Pevsner in *The buildings of England* described as 'one of the most attractive village greens in Essex'. A claim one would not dispute. The green is roughly triangular in shape. The best houses are on the south side, Aubyns, an early 16th century half-timbered house and Mundays, a 17th century plastered house with a handsome shell-hooded entrance, are shown in our photograph with the stocky tower of All Saints, rebuilt in 1802, showing just behind them.

The Green slopes down to a duck pond in the east corner, that essential element of any proper village green.

Greensted-Juxta-Ongar The church of St Andrew is one of the most remarkable buildings to survive in England. It is a log church, the nave being constructed of split oak trunks. Dendro-magnetic tests carried out in 1960 have suggested a date of 850AD for the nave timbers. Certainly the church was already standing when the body of Edmund, saint and king, rested here overnight in 1013 while on its journey from London to the shrine constructed for it at Bury St Edmunds, Suffolk. The church now stands securely, if less romantically, on a brick sill — part of the restorations of 1848. The pretty dormer windows are Tudor additions while the clapboard west tower and shingle-hung spire are of uncertain date.

The church is justly famous and correspondingly popular. Amidst all the visitors and the spruce churchyard and sparkling interior it is sometimes difficult to appreciate the extraordinary antiquity of this ancient shrine.

It is fitting that Essex, once famous for its forest and without other natural building materials should possess a wooden building of so great an age.

The King's Head, Chigwell Despite the encroachment of commuter housing estates Chigwell still gives one the sensation of a real village, the first one comes to leaving London and heading northeast. The Old King's Head is almost as picturesque today as when Dickens described it in 1841 using it as the model for the 'Maypole' in *Barnaby Rudge*. 'In the year 1775 there stood upon the border of Epping Forest, at a distance of about 12 miles from London, a house of public entertainment called the Maypole. The Maypole was an old building, with more gable ends than a lazy man would care to count on a sunny day; huge zig-zag chimneys, out of which it seemed as though even smoke could not choose but come in more than naturally fantastic shapes, imparted to it on its tortuous progress; and vast stables, gloomy, ruinous, and empty. The place was said to have been built in the days of King Henry the Eighth... with its overhanging storeys, drowsy little panes of glass, and front bulging out and projecting over the pathway. The old house looked as if it were nodding in its sleep. The brick of which it was built had originally been a deep dark red, but had grown yellow and discoloured like an old man's skin; the sturdy timbers had decayed like teeth; and here and there the ivy, like a warm garment to comfort it in its age, wrapt its green leaves closely round the time-worn walls.'

Epping Forest is almost the sole remaining tract of the once typical Essex forest scene, and even this would not have survived to us without the brave fight of Thomas Willingale of Loughton who in the mid-19th century opposed the enclosing of the forest as a result of the sale of the Crown rights. This was a royal hunting ground and some fallow deer can still be seen despite the encroachment of the roads and houses on all sides. Willingale's fight was taken up by the Corporation of London in Parliament and the courts and after 15 years the forest was declared free for the use of the people. The case for enclosure was curiously put by Coller in 1861 'The proximity of the Forest (to Loughton), and the pretext of procuring firewood by means of the loppings of the trees, which the inhabitants claim a right to cut during the winter months encourage habits of idleness and dislike of settled labour, and in some cases give occasion for poaching, all of which are injurious to the morals of the poor. Enclosures, however, seem to be commencing in the neighbourhood, which will probably check these irregular and to a certain extent, demoralising tendencies'.

But the cessation of the practice of pollarding or lopping the trees had had a most injurious effect on the forest — where once the principal tree was the hornbeam. Now the beech unchecked has taken its place and top heavy trees allow little light to pass to the forest floor beneath, where the soil becomes acid and infertile.

One ancient right of the surrounding farmers is still protected, the free grazing of cattle. Often the traffic on the busy trunk roads that bisect the forest is held up by wandering cows.

Waltham Abbey In 1030 an abbey of secular canons was founded here. A church was added by Harold and consecrated in 1060. Just over a century later the abbey was taken over by Augustinian canons and in 1184 it was elevated to the position of a 'mitred abbey' that is, it was ruled by an abbot-bishop. It quickly became one of the richest and most influential abbeys in the country. Of the church that was built by the Augustinians only the seven bays of the nave remain. These impressive great cylindrical piers with their deeply incised geometrical ornamentation are reminiscent of Durham Cathedral, the most important Early English church to have survived to us.

At the Dissolution of the Monasteries the long chancel and the transepts and crossings were all removed. The present East End arrangement of three long windows with a simple rose window above dates from the 19th century.

Nikolaus Pevsner writing in 1952 described Waltham as a little town, not yet a suburb of London, but I doubt whether he would have recognised Waltham Abbey in Tennyson's *In Memoriam*

'A single church below the Hill
Is pealing, folded in the mist'.

Now that it has suffered from such recent rapid growth and enormous increase in traffic Tennyson's illusion is even more difficult to conjure up.

Cottages at Upshire Essex enjoys no great deposits of stone for building material and was therefore reliant on timber in which, having great tracts of forest it was well endowed, and brick which made its first appearance in Britain here in Essex. Most timber frame buildings were plastered and painted. Weather-boarding is the term used for buildings, usually of timber construction, which have an outer layer of wooden boards applied either vertically or, more usually, horizontally. It affords, firstly, additional warmth and protection from the elements and, secondly, a most pleasing decorative effect.

The first appearance of this building type was in the Middle Ages but it was not until the beginning of the 17th century that it became at all widespread and most examples that we see today date from the 18th and even the 19th century.

To make any visual impact the boards must overlap. This is usually achieved by chamfering the board along the lower edge and feathering — cutting to a very thin edge along the upper. The effect created in buildings of little pretension like these cottages of Upshire is most charming.

Harlow New Town Was planned in 1947 as an overspill for London but despite the ease of communication with the capital only some 5% of the population go out of the town to work. The site chosen was in the heart of a rural community with no large centre of population to build on. Harlow Old Town and the villages of Great Parndon, Latton and Netteswell were incorporated into the New Town. The architect chosen was Frederick Gibberd who has continued to involve himself with new buildings as Harlow has grown from the original planned population of 60,000 to 80,000. The site of the town covers some 6,300 acres bounded to the north by the River Stort and the railway and on the east by the new M11. The town incorporates two industrial estates, Pinnacles on the west and Temple Fields to the east. The principal housing is arranged in four neighbourhoods lying roughly south of the Town Centre. The first to be built was Mark Hall North followed by Mark Hall South, Netteswell and finally the North West Quarter, Hare Street and Little Parndon.

Although generally considered a success in town planning terms, the four neighbourhoods are really too loosely connected and too remote from the centre for the pedestrian. The Town Centre does achieve the urban feeling required and is in fact a pedestrian precinct ringed by car parks. Sir Nikolaus Pevsner in *Buildings of England* recommends viewing the town by bicycle — sound advice.

Wendens Ambo near Saffron Walden
Originally there were two villages here, Wendens Magna and Wendens Parva. In 1662 they were united under the present name (the two Wendens). The church in our photograph was the church of Wendens Magna. Wendens Parva church has long gone. The rather short squat tower dates from Norman times and is capped with a 'Hertfordshire spike'. These cottages to the west of the church are timber-framed and like most of the village date from before 1800. The village lies close to the edge of Audley Park and came much under the influence of the powerful Howard de Walden family. Despite the national standing of its leading family, the village until comparatively recent times had remained a backwater. The coming of a railway and a village school in the 19th century began to open it up to the outside world but we learn with surprise that it was not until 1948 that electricity was brought here. Now Wendens Ambo has been discovered and the many pretty timber-framed and plastered cottages have been done up by outsiders as weekend retreats.

Audley End Thomas Audley was a lawyer of humble Essex yeoman stock. He first came to royal notice through the agency of Mary Duchess of Suffolk, the younger sister of Henry VIII, for whom he acted on local matters concerning her estates. He entered the Court circle through the patronage of Cardinal Wolsey and became a member of Parliament. There then followed a meteoric rise as he succeeded Thomas More first as Keeper of the Great Seal and then as Chancellor. He ingratiated himself with the king by passing judgement on More and by confirming the divorce of Catherine of Aragon. His obsequiousness to Henry VIII was rewarded by rich gifts in Essex. In 1536, following the Dissolution of the monasteries he was awarded St Botolphs in Colchester, the Crutched Friars in the same place, Tilty near Thaxted and, mostly magnificently, Walden Abbey. This abbey was founded by de Mandeville, the grandson of a follower of William the Conqueror, in 1136. It was most richly endowed with 117 lordships, 39 of them in Essex.

Thomas Audley died in 1544 leaving two daughters of whom only one survived to adulthood. Margaret Audley married Thomas 4th Duke of Norfolk by whom she had two sons. The elder, another Thomas, came into possession of Audley End on reaching his majority in 1582.

He was created Lord Howard de Walden by Elizabeth and in 1603, on the accession of James I, Earl of Suffolk and Lord Chamberlain. Then only did he commence the major building operations at Audley End. A subsequent owner, the third Lord Braybrooke wrote in his History of Audley End published in 1836:

'The received opinion seems to be that the Earl of Suffolk had determined, before he commenced his operations, to erect a mansion which should surpass in size and magnificence all the private residences of the kingdom: and that in aid of this design he procured a model from Italy executed in wood, at the cost of £500, some mutilated portions of which are still extant in the house.'

Three sides of the outer court have now gone and what remains is just the inner court, nothing could look less Italian than this, though it is indeed not only the greatest house in Essex but also the most magnificent of its date in the whole country.

Audley End Great Hall The Great Hall of Audley End is undoubtedly the finest room in the house, although John Evelyn gave the gallery his highest praise describing it as 'the most cheerful and I think one of the best in England'.

The Hall occupies the whole of the west range of the building. At the two ends, north and south, a pair of screens face each other. They form an extraordinary contrast to one another. The screen at the north end is a massive affair, top heavy and thickly carved with coarse motifs of paired half figures, strapwork, garlands and blank panels from the Jacobean repertoire. The second screen is of stone, as restrained as the first is prolific. There are three arches on two storeys. The arches below have coupled Tuscan pilasters between, those above Ionic pilasters. This screen and the staircase behind, leading up from the two outer arches of the screen, are the work of that individualist genius of the early 18th century Sir John Vanbrugh.

The building is in the care of the Department of the Environment who have recently completed a major programme of restoration and redecoration and it is open to the public.

Sun Inn, Saffron Walden Amongst the most precious houses in Saffron Walden are these in Church Street shown in the photograph. They date from the 14th and 15th centuries. They have an array of oversailing gables of various sizes supported on carved brackets and further enriched by moulded bressumers. The plasterwork — called pargetting — dates from the 17th century. (On one of the houses the date 1676 appears.) The decoration is a fine confusion of geometrical patterns, foliage, birds and, on the house which formerly was the Sun Inn, the figures of Thomas Hickathrift and the Wisbech Giant. Most of these houses are now let as antique shops. C. R. B. Barrett writing at the end of the 19th century disparages the Sun Inn and the rest of the group as displaying too much of the hand of the restorer, 'Though the group of buildings is sufficiently picturesque in the dusk, by daylight the illusion is dispelled'.

Saffron Walden Before the Norman conquest Saffron Walden belonged to one Ansgar whose name was recalled in the castle of Ansgar up to the 17th century. It was in the 14th century that the prefix of Saffron was added to the place name in celebration of the crocus which were grown here to produce that valuable herb, used both as a dye and as a medicine. The town was also an important centre for the wool trade and had a licence to hold a market.

The town retains many medieval timber-framed buildings as well as fine 18th century brick town houses. The church of St Mary the Virgin is one of the largest parish churches in Essex. The whole church save the crypt was rebuilt between 1450 and 1525 and shows strong connections with King's College, Cambridge and Eton College Chapel those great benefactions of Henry VI which were building at the same time. The great mason, John Wastell, who was concerned with the latter stages of the building of King's is also connected with this church.

Thaxted Town Hall The history of Thaxted dates from pre-Conquest days when the land belonged to Eluric, a Saxon thane (hence the name — Thane land') who ceded it to endow his foundation of Clare College in Suffolk. For the next 500 years (save for a brief interval in the 14th century) the two manors were bound together. In the reign of Edward III it was awarded the status and privileges of a borough. A charter from the time of Mary and Philip speaks of Thaxted as having 'had in it beyond the memory of man, a mayor etc'. In the 16th century it was one of several manors that Henry VIII settled on his first wife, Katherine of Aragon. Thus the importance of Thaxted from an early date can be judged from its aristocratic and royal connections.

In the 13th century an important trade of cutlers was established in the town and by the time of Edward III, had reached such prominence as to form a wealthy craft-guild. The size and extent of the industry can be gauged by the relics of ancient forges found as much as a mile distant from Thaxted, and the industry is recalled in at least one place name, Cutler's Green. However the cutlers were forced to abandon Thaxted eventually for want of fuel, probably in the 15th century.

In an attempt to revive the fortunes of the town one Sergeant Benlow introduced a body of weavers of cloth and fustian in the second half of the 16th century but this trade lasted scarcely half a century. An important relic remains in the old guild hall in the market place shown in our photograph here.

Thaxted Almshouse and Windmill To the south of the church stands the windmill providing a second focal point to the landscape surrounding Thaxted. This tower mill has been restored with sails, cap and fan since Pevsner visited it some 30 years ago. Between the church and windmill lie two rows of almshouses both plastered, that on the left thatched and that on the right tiled with a bargeboarded north gable.

The Essex farmland though now so greatly valued suffered like the rest of the country in the 19th century. A survey carried out in 1834 by the Poor Law commission showed that few farm labourers could support a family of four children without parish assistance, and then only when the diet comprised mainly bread and potatoes. The provision of an almshouse from a more affluent age was indeed a boon to the sick and elderly though a contemporary description of this type of housing paints a less rosy picture of the traditional thatched cottage with honeysuckle round the door.

Essex Standard Jan 18, 1850

'Great numbers of these cottages are situated in low and damp situations and their heavy and grass covered thatches appear as if they had almost crushed the buildings down into the earth. Little or no light can ever find its way into the wretched little windows many of which are more than half stopped up with rags and pieces of paper. In point of fact there are many of them which but for the possession of a chimney would be nothing superior to many of the most wretched cabins which I have witnessed in Tipperary and many other parts of Ireland.'

Finchingfield This 'Beau Ideal' of an English village must be one of the most familiar views in Essex. The scene is the quintessence of English rural life, the wide village green where the stream, a tributary of the river Pant opens into a little pond, the row of whitewashed cottages with warm red tiled roofs and at the top of the little hill the squat Norman west tower of the village church, St John. The tower is capped gracefully if a little incongruously by an 18th century cupola.

The advantages of the site are as immediately apparent to us as they must have been to its Saxon founders, Fincs folk, from whom it takes its name. The hill, steep by East Anglian standards, offered a naturally defensible situation while the stream at its foot provided an ample water supply.

On the village street in front of the church is a long low timber-framed cottage plastered and painted white, this was the former hall of the religious and charitable guild of the Holy Trinity. A gateway through this building leads from the street into the churchyard.

Opposite the Guildhall is a row of almshouses endowed by Sir Robert Kemp whose family built Spainshall at the end of the 16th century. This house lies just north of the village. It is an appealing red brick, many gabled building with the irregular façade of our native architecture before it met with the regularising influence of the Rennaissance.

Dunmow Old Town Hall Dunmow is an attractive small town and its pond and pretty village houses around it make a charming group. Dunmow is famous for its bacon, notably its 'Flitch'. The 'Flitch' is a side of bacon which is offered to any couple who can prove they have not had a quarrel in the preceding year. The custom was established in the 13th century by Robert Fitzwalter, one of the barons who held King John at Runnymede and forced him to sign the Magna Carta. The custom survived to this day, though it was in danger of disappearing with the closure some years ago of the last bacon curer in the town. In 1983 a new bacon business started up and promises to continue to observe the custom. The presentation is made at an annual fair held in late summer.

The half-timbered Old Town Hall seen with overhang stands at the corner of the Market Place. It was no doubt in this building that as the parish records of 1850 state 'a large amount of public business connected with the petty sessions, the Board of Guardians and the Public taxes is transacted'. The activity was created by people protesting at the erection of a toll gate at the south end of the High Street which, they claimed, would penalise those coming to Dunmow as a public duty as well as 'many persons who are in the daily habit of coming into it from the south'. Dunmow is now even more of a road junction as the main A120 on which it stands links Colchester and Braintree with the M11.

Old School, Felstead Hard against the churchyard stands the old school house timber framed and plastered with an overhanging upper floor. Next to it is the former headmaster's house. The school was founded in the 16th century by the infamous Richard Rich who through the betrayal of his friends and patrons rose to become Chancellor and in recognition of his ruthless pursuit of his own advantage was awarded Leez Priory at the Dissolution of the monasteries.

This building antedates even the school having started as a medieval guildhall. The school itself is now more commodiously housed in a tall dark brick structure topped by a tower and gable and dressed with blue bricks to make the whole effect gloomier still. Despite its unprepossessing architecture the school has a high reputation and the standing of a public school. One former pupil at least managed to throw off his provincial origins as a fellow alumnus records in a letter to his parents from Cambridge in 1815.

'There is a man here, a famous mail-driver, foxhunter etc. etc who goes about college and into lectures in a green coat and red waistcoat, an established Buck whom I to my no small astonishment discovered to be an old friend of mine, by name Lippyatt formerly of Felsted, but am happy he has not recognised me.'

Cressing Temple Barns near Braintree In 1135 the Knights Templars were granted the Manor of Cressing which forthwith adopted the additional name of Temple in recognition of this connection. The Templars were, according to opposing standpoints, either greedy warlike men of little principle who milked the poor in the name of God and the protection of the Holy Land or the heroic band of soldier monks dedicated to the protection of the birthplace of Christianity whose success was attributable to the efficient running of their order. However there is no doubt they were wealthy enough to attract the attention of the king who in 1312 ordered their suppression. Cressing Temple manor, with others, then passed into the hands of their rivals, the Knights Hospitallers, with whom it remained until the beginning of the 16th century. There are three great barns at Cressing. The earliest two date from the ownership of the Templars and are therefore nearly 700 years old. The first was the weather-boarded Barley Barn, built by the Templars as soon as they took possession. The brick built Wheat Barn was added towards the end of the 13th century and is slightly larger measuring an impressive 140ft long by 40ft high. The smallest and latest is whitewashed and built in 1623. The whole group is most beautiful and impressive. Still in private hands they can be visited on written application to the owners.

Witham The town of Witham is divided by the railway. North of the railway is the older part called Chippinghill, an ancient village arranged around a triangular green which lies on the side of a hill and at the apex of the triangle stands the church of St Nicholas. South of the railway is the comparatively modern town based on the High Street and adjoining streets. The church dates almost entirely from the 14th century. The grey west tower shows above the irregular tile roofs and weatherbeaten gables interspersed with clusters of brick chimneys. The groups of houses around the green of Chippinghill are most picturesque, many of them are timber framed and some pargetted but in between are some grander 18th century brick fronted houses.

Earthworks near Chippinghill are supposedly the site of a burgh built by King Edward the Elder, and indicate a date of around 913 for the first settlement here.

Halstead — Courtauld Weaving Mill

Halstead has been a centre of the cloth trade since the middle ages. The cloth production was organised by a clothier. The spinners and weavers worked at home in one of the neighbouring villages and the cloth was then fulled and finished centrally and dispatched to London for export. The principal markets for the Essex cloth were Italy and Portugal. The industry which had been in decline throughout the 18th century was finally ruined by the Napoleonic wars which frustrated much of the trade with Europe.

Courtauld's, originally established at Pedmarsh, rejuvenated the industry when it moved its silk manufactury here at the end of the 18th century. The whole of the large town of Halstead is now much involved with the firm.

There was something of a hiccup in the good relations of the town and its adopted industry when in 1836 Courtauld's introduced steam driven machinery. The 'Essex Independent' of 12 November 1836 records 'a great outcry is made against Messrs Courtauld and Taylor for having introduced into their manufactories additional machinery which may throw out of employment some of the weavers. We sympathise with those who may thus lose employment, but it must be recollected that it is by the perfection of our machinery alone that England can expect to maintain the proud position which she occupies'.

The factory is still grouped around the nucleus of the handsome weather-boarded mill, built by Courtaulds when they first moved here.

Castle Hedingham A landmark in the low north Essex scenery for miles around, the keep of Hedingham Castle is one of the finest of its date still surviving in England. Built in 1140 it is contemporary with Rochester and only slightly later than the White Tower of the Tower of London. It was built by the Lords de Vere, Earls of Oxford, one of the most powerful families to have accompanied the Conqueror to Britain. Later de Vere's were somewhat unhappy in their allegiances. The castle was besieged and taken early in the 13th century by King John's supporters, no friends of the de Vere's. At the end of the 14th century the ninth Earl, a favourite of Richard II, followed his master into exile. The de Vere's supported the Lancastrian during the Wars of the Roses and thus suffered attainder and exile. Finally with the triumph of Henry of Richmond, later Henry VII, their luck changed and the 13th Earl, John, was sworn a privy councillor, Constable of the Tower and appointed Lord High Admiral of England, Ireland and the Duchy of Aquitaine. The de Vere's star rose higher still when Henry VIII restored to them the office of Great Chamberlain. Too much emboldened by this mark of favour, the Earl greeted Henry VIII on a visit to Hedingham Castle with such a show of liveried attendants that he breached the Status of Retainers, an Act passed in order to curtail the large private armies kept by powerful barons, and the king caused him to be fined the unprecedented sum of 15,000 marks. The history of the Earls of Oxford ends with the 20th Earl who left an only child, a daughter. She married Charles Beauclerk the natural son of Charles II by Nell Gwynn whose descendants take as secondary title to the Duke of St Albans that of Baron Vere.

The castle itself survived in a complete condition no longer than the last earl who in 1666, during the Dutch War, in order to prevent Hedingham being billeted with soldiers or being made a prison for the captured Dutch soldiers, caused the keep to be partly dismantled and brought to the condition we see it in today.

The Great Hall, shown in our photograph must surely be the finest surviving domestic interior of its date in England. It forms the whole of the second floor of the keep and is approached by a staircase in the northwest angle tower. Half way up the walls it is encircled by a gallery the openings to which echo the window embrasures below. The fireplace is decorated in typical Norman style with zig-zag as are other of the arches and columns.

This remarkable building is opened to the public by the owner who lives in the early 18th century house embraced by the eastern portion of the outer building.

Bulmer Brickworks Roman bricks found in the walls of the parish church here suggest that Bulmer might have had a brickfield some 2,000 years ago. With the departure of the Romans in the fifth century brickmaking seems to have ceased but the great durability of the flat Roman bricks made them an important item of salvage from all ruined Roman buildings. Until Tudor times bricks were little used in England for major building and brickmaking did not recommence at Bulmer on any scale until the 16th century.

Nowadays the Bulmer brickworks are of more than local importance. The hand made bricks produced are in constant demand for the restoration of historic brick buildings where it is essential to match not only the colour but also the texture of the existing bricks. Recently Bulmer has provided bricks for the restoration of Hampton Court.

The bricks are baked in the kiln, shown in our photograph, in batches of 12,000 and baking takes seven days. In achieving the necessary temperatures of 1,200C, the seven fires surrounding the kiln consume six tons of coal and Tom Bird, the foreman of the Bulmer brickworks, has been stoking the kiln since 1953.

Before the use of coal there were great variations in the colours of bricks from a single kiln because the temperature varied with the type of wood used. Different colours are obtained nowadays by controlling the amount of air admitted to the kiln in the later stages of firing.

The River Stour at Lamarsh The River Stour forms the northern boundary of Essex between the village of Sturmer and the sea. It is important to remember that this most ravishing valley belongs to Essex as well as to Suffolk. It is undoubtedly the most appealing part of the Essex landscape and is particularly precious as it served as the continual inspiration to the greatest painter of English landscape, John Constable. It is rich fertile farming country busy with growing things. Here is no wild rugged beauty but the quiet memorable loveliness we long for when far from home.

Michael Drayton in *Polyolbion*, written in 1622, expresses his admiration in more heroic terms.

'Great Claps and shouts were heard resounding to the shore
Wherewith the Essexian nymphs applaud their loved Stour.'

Lamarsh church is worth a visit. The Norman tower is one of the six round towers of Essex, a form most suited to construction in local flint.

Wormingford Mill Wormingford lies in the lovely Stour valley, between Dedham and Sudbury and boasts a number of fine 15th and 16th century buildings, notably Church House which has a most distinctive gable. In more troubled times the Stour was a considerable barrier to military movement and near this place the 9th Roman Legion was cut off and massacred when marching to relieve the garrison at Colchester beseiged by Boadicea. The alarums and excursions of the Middle Ages led to the construction of moats round several houses in the neighbourhood notably Rotchfords, a timber framed and plastered farmhouse dating from the 15th century, but also Wood Hall and Smallbridge Hall, the last just over the county boundary in Suffolk.

In the 16th century the Stour was navigable as far as Sudbury and mills like the one seen here, the one at Dedham and the one owned by Constable's father at Flatford sent their flour by barge to Mistly quay from whence it would be dispatched to London. Scenes of the Essex landscape in the early 19th century are familiar to us from the paintings of John Constable, especially his celebrated painting of *Flatford Mill* which shows barges being worked on the Stour. Wormingford Mill itself ceased to be used in the early years of this century and the wheel was dismantled when in the 1920s it became the home of John Nash, another painter of the East Anglian scene.

Dedham High Street lies just a quarter of a mile from the county boundary with Suffolk. This most attractive small town bears comparison with the well-endowed Suffolk villages of Lavenham and Long Melford. Like these neighbours its wealth dates back to the 14th century when, under Edward III, Flemish weavers arrived to instruct the locals in their skills and enable them to capitalise on the wool production of the region. The prosperity of the area reached its climax in the following century, the greatest monument to it being the wonderful churches built with the money provided by wealthy burghers anxious for the welfare of their immortal souls. Dedham church was built principally with endowments from two local merchant families, the Gurdons and the Webbes. On the ground floor of the tower can be seen the initials and merchant marks of the Webbes. The whole church, including the mighty west tower standing 130ft high, was completed in the space of 30 years — all of one style — in 1520. As at East Bergholt, the ground floor of the tower is open through from north to south as a processional way.

The High Street itself is a charming mixture of half-timbered, plastered and brick houses. The majority date from the 16th and 17th century while Dedham was still enjoying its prosperity.

Two Georgian brick façades deserve attention. Firstly the grammar school just east of the church and secondly Shermans on the north side of High Street facing the church. Although the 18th century witnessed the decline in prosperity of all the Essex towns whose wealth was based on wool, things had not come to such a pass as to exclude all frivolity. The *Ipswich Journal* gives us an agreeable insight into country pleasures at this date: Dedham, 23 October 1745:

'Our peal of Eight Bells being now compleated, Friday the First of November is fixed for Ringing them, when we believe they will be esteemed good Bells.

NB In the Long Room at the Sun, in the evening, will be country dancing; proper musick is provided.'

Mistley Quay near Manningtree Mistley lies on the south side of the Stour estuary just where it bellies out to over a mile in width.

In the mid 18th century a maltings was established here. Philip Morant in his *History of Essex*, 1768, speaks of 30 brick houses, granaries, warehouses, a large malting office and quays. These maltings share with Snape the honour of being the largest and finest group in East Anglia. They also support one of the country's largest herds of swans which since the decline in the activity of the maltings have suffered a fall in their numbers. Here massed in the evening light they look most splendid against the industrial backdrop of the cranes and quayside. The estuary is largely clogged with tidal mud through which a narrow stream winds, little used save by small-boat sailors. The quiet mud flats provide an ideal habitat for thousands of waders and wild fowl many of which in winter are visitors from ice-bound northern shores.

Mistley Towers, near Manningtree Mr Richard Rigby MP, son of a factor who had made a fortune out of the 'South Sea Bubble' speculation, achieved great prominence and in 1768 George III made him Paymaster General of the Forces. His father had already built a new village here of brick houses, warehouses and a quay to further the grain trade from the rich Essex hinterland, and the son formed the grander plan of converting Mistley into a fashionable spa.

To the house built by his father he added a picturesque landscape park abounding in Chinese and Gothic follies which is described by William Hurn in *Heath Hill*:

'Pleas'd could I, Mistley thro' the hamlet stray
where the green park unveils the grass-rob'd way
and pleas'd depict the beauties that surround
Thy lovely structure on the smooth-mown ground.'

Then in 1774 he called in Robert Adam to build a 'bagno' — that is a saltwater bath. This was designed but never actually built. Adam added to the church two square towers at the north and south ends (ritual west and east) and porticoes against the ritual north and south sides. The whole church, except for the towers, was pulled down and another church built nearby. The towers are composed of wholly secular elements, freestanding Tuscan columns, entablature, square storey with four pediments surmounted by tall slim drums with attached Ionic columns and crowned by a dome. Perhaps the Mistley example explains why this greatest of British architects enjoyed so few church commissions!

Colchester Castle Camulodumum, the capital of the Trinobantes, was conquered by Claudius in AD 44. Following a defeat at the hands of Boadicea the Romans walled the town in AD 65, and large sections of these walls still appear between the streets of houses. The walls enclosed an area of some 108 acres, smaller certainly than London, Cirencester, St Albans and Wroxeter but quite possibly more densely populated. The Great West Gate called the Balkerne gate is the sole survivor of the four gates leading in each compass direction. The Royal Commission on Historical Monuments listed 92 Roman buildings within the walls and many of the impressive remains found by archaelogists including several tesselated and mosaic pavements are now exhibited in the Castle Museum.

The castle stands on a site close to the Roman Forum. It dates from the end of the 11th century and was a royal possession. It measures 151ft by 11ft and is the largest keep in existence, surpassing even the mighty White Tower in size. The exterior walls were formerly faced in septaria stone and tile though this has now fallen away almost everywhere to reveal the rubble core. The castle was several times besieged during the turbulent reign of King John, but with the comparative stability of the country in the following century the castle passed into private hands and was used as a prison. The most noteworthy captives to be held here were Sir Thomas Malory, who wrote the ultimate eulogy of chivalry *Le Morte d'Arthur*, James Parnell the Quaker who starved himself to death here and many Marian martyrs, for Colchester was heavily punished for having espoused the New Religion with fervour.

The keep is now only two storeys high. A further two upper storeys were taken down by a building speculator named Wheely who bought the castle to plunder for building material after the Restoration of Charles II. Happily his efforts were curtailed before he managed to raze the keep. The castle now belongs to the Corporation of Colchester and possesses one of the finest archaelogical museums in the country.

Colchester Siege House That popular nursery character 'Olde King Cole' was, according to legend, king of Colchester and father of St Helena. She married a Roman general who took her to Rome where she gave birth to Constantine, the first Christian emperor.

Gurney Benham's poem *King Cole of Colchester* gives further biographical details of the legendary father of St Helena and this description of his kingdom:

> He reigned in a town which all men know
> Where the Cornfields wave, and the roses blow
> And the dainty, delicate oysters grow,
> to add to its fame and Glory.

This idyllic description of 'Britain's Oldest Recorded Town' may seem to us only a small part of the picture. Certainly Colchester has been much fought over in its 2,000 years of existence. Boadicea led a successful raid against the Romans during their occupation and briefly ousted them. At the beginning of the 13th century the barons took the castle which was held in the name of King John, and garrisoned the castle with French knights who scurvily betrayed their English comrades and yielded the castle once again to the king. During the Civil War the city was besieged once more. In 1648 it was held by two royalist knights, Sir Charles Lucas and Sir George Lisle. The bombardment from Fairfax leading the parliamentarian forces was ferocious and traces of the consequent devastation are still visible today. St Botolph's Priory was perhaps the greatest loss. Surviving the Dissolution to become a parish church, it was knocked to pieces by the parliamentarian artillery fire. At the Dissolution, the second monastic foundation, St John's passed to the Lucas family, who plundered it for building material for their new mansion. This house was unhappily fortified by Sir Charles Lucas in preparation for the Civil War siege and was completely destroyed on Fairfax's orders after the surrender.

The Siege House stands near the old East Gate, a 15th century half-timbered house, oversailing and gabled, though much restored, its ancient timbers still bear the marks of Fairfax's artillery fire.

Bourne Mill Bourne Mill stands on Bourne Brook, a tributary of the River Colne. The first mill on this site was built on land granted to the Monks of St John's in 1096. The brook was dammed to provide a sufficient flow of water to work the mill and incidently provide a stew pond where the monks could store fish for the days of Abstinence. At the dissolution of the monasteries the Abbey of St John's, with the land pertaining to it, was granted to the Lucas family. The present building was erected in 1591, by Sir Thomas Lucas as a fishing lodge, the date is inscribed on a stone set high up on the south gable. The ravishing curly gables topped with a multiplicity of obelisks and pinnacles show the exuberant display beloved of the Elizabethans.

At the end of the 16th century many Flemish refugess arrived in Colchester. They established the famous manufacture of baize which continued to bring prosperity to the town for the next two centuries. The Lucas family let the mill to 'Bay-Makers' while keeping the fishing rights for themselves. Two important processes in the manufacture of baize were carried out here, the first was spinning the yarn, the second, at the end of the process was fulling the cloth. When the Bay-Trade failed, at the beginning of the 19th century Bourne Mill became a flour mill. The weather-boarded hoist lift was added at this time to take up the huge grain sacks and at the same time the machinery invaded the ground floor room of the fishing lodge.

The mill was presented to the National Trust, by an anonymous donor in 1936. The Trust has now restored much of the mill machinery to working order and the mill is open to the public.

Layer Marney Towers The Marneys were a Norman family whose name first appeared in the time of Henry II but they achieved no great advancement until Henry VIII took up Henry Marney, 'a scant well born gentleman of no grete lande.' He was elevated by his patron to be a Knight of the Garter and a Peer, and, in 1523 only a few months before his death, he was made keeper of the Great Seal. At this time the building of his house at Layer Marney was in full swing. The work at Layer Marney continued under Henry's son John but when he too died only two years later, the last of the male line of Marneys, building work stopped. This left the Great Tower with little to balance it of what was planned to be a great courtyard house with the tower placed centrally on the north side as a gatehouse.

Although for more than 80 years before the building of Layer Marney domestic buildings of this type had served no defensive purpose, the gatehouse was still the most popular form of display. At the time of its building this tower at Layer Marney was the tallest so far constructed but it also exceeded all its predecessors in the beauty and accomplishment of its ornamentation. It shows one of the earliest examples of the use of moulded terracotta in England. The moulds were imported direct from Italy and show the full repertoire of stock Renaissance forms, though their implementation here is still entirely Gothic. Thus the trefoil cusping on the windows is formed by the outline of dolphin scrolls.

With the demise of the last two Marneys the house went through a succession of owners until at the end of the 18th century it was left to fall into decay. Nearly a century passed before the first, ill advised restoration programme was begun. This first attempt was halted by lack of funds and a more sympathetic approach was achieved by the next owner, Mr de Zoete who desired a suitable setting for his impressive collection of early furniture. The house, though still privately owned is open regularly to the public.

Tollesbury is almost a little town rather than a village. It lies on the north bank of the Blackwater close to its mouth. This area of wide mud banks and shallow tidal waters is a popular habitat for all wild fowl and from the 16th century it has been a renowned sporting paradise providing large quantities of wild duck, mallard, teal and widgeon. Daniel Defoe in his tour through the eastern counties offers a warning to the London sportsmen travelling to the Essex coast.

'But it must be remembered, too, that the gentlemen who are such lovers of the sport, and go so far for it, often return with an Essex ague on their backs, which they find a heavier load than the fowls they have shot.'

Tollesbury at the end of the 19th century was also famous for its oyster beds.

Now the town gains its renown and popularity from the sailing community who frequent the inland waters of this part of the Essex coast. These great barn-like, weather-boarded buildings are stood up upon stone and brick plinths to keep them dry during a high tide. They must of necessity stand close to the water for within is a complicated system of pulleys and racks to hang up the wet sails to allow them to dry. The wooden shutters are opened in fine drying weather to accelerate the process.

View to Bradwell Point from West Mersea
Mersea Island lies at the mouth of two navigable rivers the Colne and the Blackwater, and thus in the days of frequent Danish invasions it became a place of strategic importance. In 894 Alfred made a stand here against the Danes but little more was heard of the island until the mid 16th century, when a complaint was made that the pay of the Blockhouse Captain and soldiers at East Mersea was in arrears. Whether the island had been continuously fortified during the intervening 750 years seems uncertain. In 1648 the small garrison was defeated by the parliamentary forces who took possession of the island. A military presence was maintained here until the Restoration when shortage of money forced the closing of the outlying military posts.

Now the island is chiefly remarkable for its excellent oyster beds and as a popular holiday spot. At low tide the island is joined to the main land by an ancient causeway, The Strood.

Our photograph shows a view south across the mouth of the Blackwater estuary with in the distance the great squat bulk of the Bradwell atomic power station.

Wivenhoe near Colchester A village more than half devoted to the water, Wivenhoe stands on the east side of the River Colne, and was formerly linked by a ferry to Fingringhoe. The quay presents a busy scene of boat yards and small sailing craft and a jumble of attractive cottages and houses.

In the 18th century this was the scene of much stealthy activity as smugglers landed rich cargoes of French wines and brandy for the consumption of the neighbouring gentry. The tale is told through the records of the Harwich Collector of Customs:

'6 Oct 1777 Having been informed by undoubted authority that there are upwards of thirty sail of small cutters constantly employed in smuggling between the Naze point and the south of the Thames, which vessels easily elude the pursuit of the *Argus* and the *Bee* cutters stationed at this point by running over the sands where on account of their great draft of water those cutters dare not follow, by which means they escape and carry on with impunity a great trade in the rivers and creeks which abound in these parts.'

In the next couple of years the Excise officers began to have some success against the smugglers as an impressive list of the seizures made by the two cutters shows. But help was not always forthcoming. Many people enjoyed the contraband goods, as the following account, from the same source records:
8 March 1779 'We take this occasion of informing your honours that a large cutter of near 200 tons, mounting 14 four-pounders and 47 men, belonging to one Wenham but commanded by a man nicknamed "Swipes", well known as a notorious smuggler upon this coast, has lately made it a practice to bring a very large cargo of contraband goods which she lands in Colne and Burnham rivers as fast as she can perform the voyages between Flushing and this coast. Neither of the cutters stationed at this port are in any way a match for her, but we had a plan to endeavour to take her if we had the assistance of about 40 soldiers of the 25th Regiment quartered at this place, but on applying to the commanding officer for that purpose he informed us that he had particular orders not to furnish any men to assist any officers of the Revenue'.

Brightlingsea It is almost completely surrounded by water. It lies at the mouth of the Colne estuary and enjoys the peculiar distinction of being a member of the Cinque Ports. It is the only member of the confederation to lie north of the Thames, and is a member by virtue of being a limb of Sandwich, one of the original five ports. The confederation was formed before the Norman conquest, a successor to the Roman coastal defence system formed to repulse Saxon invasion. The original five ports were Hastings, New Romney, Hythe, Dover and Sandwich. They were re-formed by William the Conqueror and at some time after this Winchelsea and Rye were added. In return for commercial and judicial privileges the Cinque Ports were bound to provide ships for the king's fleet.

The town is disappointing architecturally, not so the Church of Brightlingsea which stands some way from the town centre, and reflects the wealth of the town during the 15th century. One monument requires particular attention. Nicholas Mugens, a German grew rich in London in the insurance business. He is reputed to have died worth £100,000. His indebtedness to the sea is shown by a relief of ships. A globe is supported on the left by a winged female figure on the right, a putto bearing a cornucopia which spills out not only fruit but also coins.

Brightlingsea is bound to the south and east by a creek where at low tide herons fish the muddy channels. Now they must share these calm waters with these sail boarders.

St Osyth's Priory St Osyth was the daughter of Frithwald, 1st Christian King of the Angles. She founded a nunnery at this place. In October 653 it was besieged by a band of Danes. She refused to worship their gods and was ordered to be executed. On the spot where she was martyred a clear fountain sprang out which reputedly was a cure for many ills.

At the beginning of the 12th century a Priory of Augustinian Canons was founded here and of this earliest building a few fragments dating from 1118 remain.

The gatehouse was added in the third quarter of the 15th century and is the finest survival of the monastic buildings. It is beautifully faced in panels of flint and stone. Originally the central niche was occupied by a statue of St Osyth flanked by SS Peter and Paul. In the spandrels of the central archway there are reliefs of St Michael and the Dragon. Within the archway is a lierne vault, the bosses boldly carved with heads of saints and other religious devices. The last Abbot, John Vyntoner added the great 16 light oriel window in the abbots' lodging beneath which is a double row of finely carved shields.

After the Dissolution of the monasteries the abbey remained in royal hands until 1553 when it was granted to John first Lord Darcy. It was he who built the great tower and the chequer board block. He lies buried in the church, his effigy lies on a tomb chest a foot above his wife. They are dressed in contemporary clothes, their hands folded in prayer, the whole most beautifully executed.

The house is privately owned and opened to the public.

Clacton-on-Sea Clacton was developed as a seaside resort in the 1870s, that is, after Walton and before Frinton. Always more populous than either of the two resorts to its north it is now more than twice the size of both of them put together.

Its celebrated pier was built in 1873 the pavilion was added 20 years later.

A contemporary description of Clacton from the *Halstead Times* of 19 June 1875 gives us a heady picture of the town at the outset of its popularity:

'Extensive improvements have been made in this watering-place since last year.... Handsome residences have sprung up in all directions, and the town, as viewed from the pier, now presents a general outline of the plan originally laid down by the promoters of the undertaking. Those who remember what the place was a few years ago would hardly recognise it now. The cliffs to the north of the pier are now surmounted by clusters of neatly designed houses, flanked by the Royal Hotel... the pier, which is 500ft long, will be lengthened another 500ft at the end of the season.'

The Royal Hotel was three years old at the time this description was written. It is in the informal style of seaside architecture, a long white stucco façade with a showy ironwork verandah on the first floor.

The whole scene is now greatly enlivened, beyond the sedate imaginings of those early promoters, by the huge permanent funfair.

Harwich — Treadmill Crane A glance at the map will easily explain the importance of Harwich in naval terms. It lies on a narrow peninsula which forms the southern side of the estuaries of the Stour and Orwell. The harbour is protected from the ravages of the North Sea by a tongue of land on the Suffolk side now occupied by Felixstowe. The town was planted here around 1200 by Roger Bigod, Earl of Norfolk on land belonging to his manor of Dovercourt. The town was laid out on a strict grid iron pattern, the three main roads running diagonally north west. They are still there today, West Street, Middle Street (now Church Street) and East or High Street (now King's Head Street). These were traversed by narrower streets with staggered crossings to frustrate the most biting elements of the northeast wind. The church of St Nicholas (rebuilt in 1821) was a Chapel of Dovercourt. In 1253 a licence was granted for a market to be held there. In 1318 Edward II awarded it its own charter and in 1352 it was walled.

The Hundred Year's War brought great prosperity to the ports on the East Anglian coast, the dockyards were kept continually occupied in building and refitting boats and sharp minded fishermen could make a decent profit in compensation for the use of their boats to carry provisions to the army in Bordeaux while the ballast of wine they returned with was additional inducement to forego the uncertainties of fishing the North Sea.

The Navy kept a dockyard here until comparatively recent times. The crane shown in our photograph now standing on the Green was moved when a new jetty was planned to be built on the site of the former Naval Dockyard. The crane house is weather-boarded. Within are tread-wheels which were designed to be worked by men.

Harwich — Trinity House Depot Trinity House was first granted a charter in 1514 to regulate pilotage of shipping. During the following century the concerns of Trinity House became so diverse that it is difficult to identify any maritime activity in which they were not engaged. Now they are responsible for three important areas of operation; firstly they are the general lighthouse authority for England, Wales, the Channel Islands and Gibraltar, providing lighthouses, light vessels, buoys and beacons as aids to navigation; secondly they are responsible for pilotage in 40 districts of the United Kingdom, including, most importantly the busy routes of London and the Thames; finally they are a charitable organisation providing and maintaining homes for elderly mariners and their dependents.

The major east coast depot is at Harwich, which is the largest of the six Trinity House depots. The district covers the whole area from Berwick-on-Tweed to Lyme Bay and maintains 32 lighthouses, 12 beacons and 13 minor lights. The lighthouses are served by four lighthouse tenders. Three of them, THVs *Siren*, *Mermaid* and *Patricia* are stationed at Harwich. The last is the flagship of the Trinity House fleet. In addition there are in the East Coast district some 480 buoys both lighted and unlighted. Of the 640 Trinity House pilots 415 are employed in the London district, the heaviest commitment on the service, and of these 111 work out of Harwich. The service provides pilots not only to London ports but also to the East Coast ports of Felixstowe, Harwich, Parkeston, Ipswich, Mistley, Colchester and the River Blackwater.

The depot is situated on the waterfront at Harwich and comprises the buoy yard, shown in our photograph, workshops and service stores as well as an office building for the administration of the service.

The whole service is maintained without assistance from The Taxpayer.

List of Plates

Audley End — Great Hall 52
              West View 50

Bradwell — Church 28
           Point 98
           St Peter's Chapel 26
Brightlingsea 102
Bulmer Brickworks 76
Burnham-on-Crouch 24

Chelmsford 32
Chigwell 38
Clacton-on-Sea 106
Colchester — Bourne Mill 92
           Castle 88
           Siege House 90
Cressing Old Barn 68

Dedham 82
Dunmow 64

Epping Forest 40

Felstead, Old School 66
Finchingfield 62

Great Warley 18
Greensted 36

Hadleigh Castle 20
Halstead 72
Harlow 46

Harwich — Treadmill Crane 108
         Trinity House Depot 110
Hedingham Castle 74

Lamarsh 78
Layer Marney Towers 94

Maldon 30
Mistley — Quay 84
        Towers 86

Rainham Hall 12

St Osyth 104
Saffron Walden — High Street 56
                Sun Inn 54
Shellhaven 16
Silvertown 10
Southend-on-Sea 22
Stratford Watermills 8

Thaxted — Almshouses 60
         Town Hall 58
Tilbury Fort 14
Tollesbury 96

Upshire 44

Waltham Abbey 42
Wendens Ambo 48
Witham Village 70
Wivenhoe 100
Wormingford Mill 80
Writtle Village Green 34

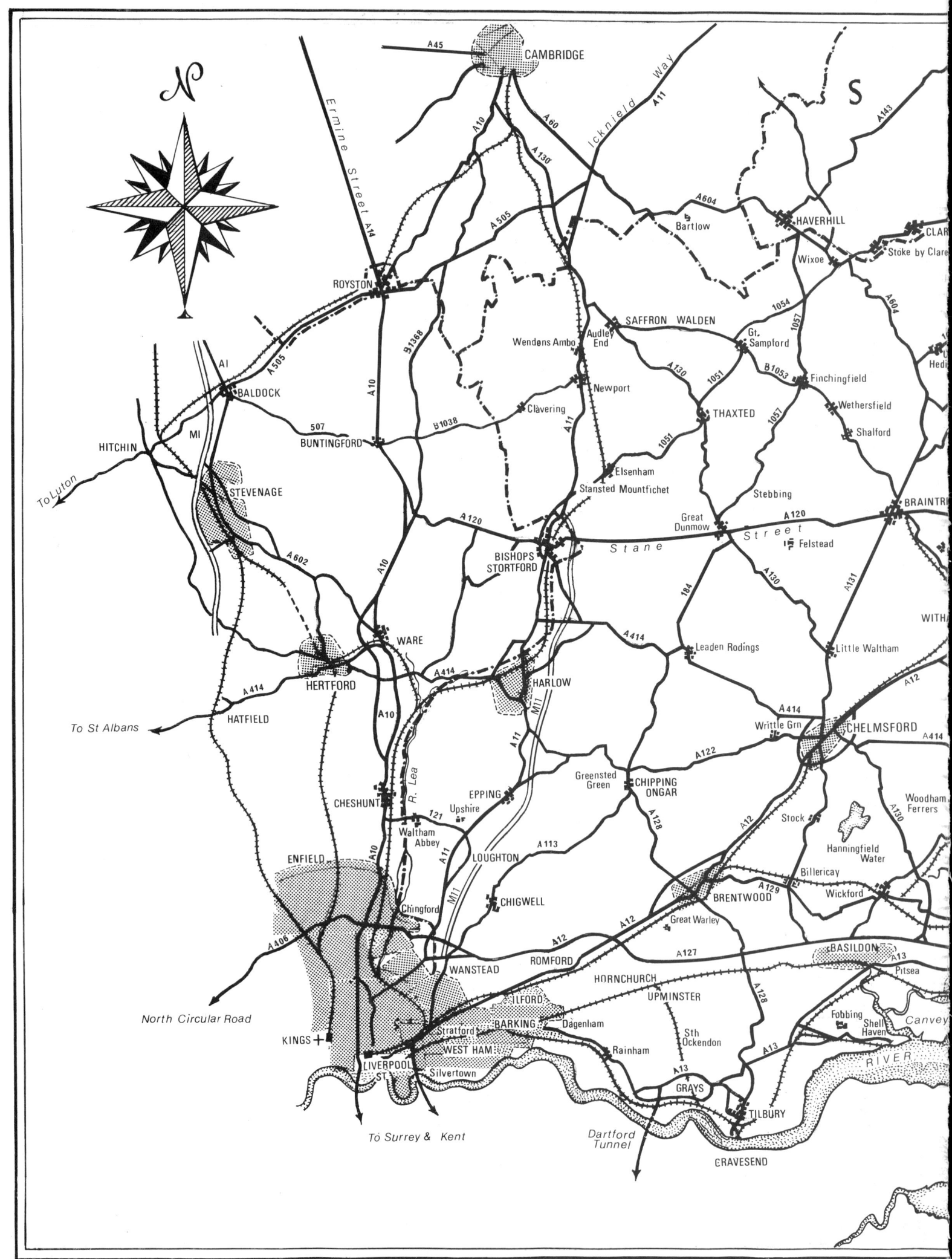